INFLUENCING CHILDREN
to become
WORLD CHANGERS

JOY DAWSON

THOMAS NELSON PUBLISHERS®
Nashville

A *Division of Thomas Nelson, Inc.*
www.ThomasNelson.com

Published in Nashville, Tennessee, by Thomas Nelson, Inc.

Unless otherwise marked, all scriptures are taken from the NEW KING JAMES VERSION. Copyright © 1979, 1980, 1982, Thomas Nelson, Inc.

Scriptures marked TLB are taken from THE LIVING BIBLE (Wheaton, IL: Tyndale House Publishers, 1971).

Scriptures marked AMP are taken from THE AMPLIFIED BIBLE: Old Testament. Copyright © 1962, 1964 by Zondervan Publishing House; and from THE AMPLIFIED NEW TESTAMENT. Copyright © 1958 by the Lockman Foundation.

Scripture quotations noted NIV are taken from the HOLY BIBLE, NEW INTERNATIONAL VERSION®. Copyright© 1973,1978,1984 by International Bible Society. Used by permission of Zondervan Bible Publishing House. All rights reserved.

The "NIV" and "New International Version" trademarks are registered in the United States Patent and Trademark Office by International Bible Society. Use of either trademark requires the permission of International Bible Society.

Scripture quotations noted KJV are from The Holy Bible, KING JAMES VERSION.

Library of Congress Cataloging-in-Publication Data

Dawson, Joy.
    Influencing children to become world changers / Joy Dawson.
      p. cm.
    ISBN 0-7852-6364-0
    1. Christian education—Home training. 2. Christian education
of children. 3. Discipling (Christianity). I. Title.
    BV1590.D39 2003
    248.8'45—dc21   200201569

Printed in the United States of America

03 04 05 06 07 BVG 6 5 4 3 2 1

ACKNOWLEDGMENTS

I am deeply grateful to the Holy Spirit, who has been my greatest source of inspiration and revelation while writing this book, and I delight to give the credit where it belongs.

My beloved, lifelong partner and best friend, Jim, has done the computer work from my handwritten scripts. I am very grateful for his encouragement and practical help.

My grateful thanks also goes to those who contributed their vital testimonies.

And it has been a delight to work with Victor Oliver, Kristen Lucas, and Beth Clark of Thomas Nelson Publishers.

CONTENTS

FOREWORD

There are many wonderful books on the market which cover the subject of how to successfully raise children. This book is not intended to add to that list. Rather, it is an attempt to present some Biblical priorities in the lives of those involved in discipling children—Biblical priorities that will influence them to rise above the average and make a difference in their generation.

I don't profess to have all the answers. I am learning all the time. But what I share in the following pages really works.

MENTORING BY EXAMPLE

S o you've been entrusted with the responsibility of influencing children! You can approach it in one of two ways—either by enduring the ordeal, longing for the day when they're old enough to be off your hands; or by seeing the assignment as a fantastic opportunity to help the little tykes become world changers, history makers and shapers in their generation. Perspective makes the difference.

Someone has to have the privilege of helping to shape the lives of future outstanding scientists, doctors, government leaders, national and international spiritual leaders, missionary statesmen and pioneers, Nobel Peace Prize winners, brilliant philosophers and writers whose works shape the thinking of millions . . . and the list goes on. Why not you?

We must never underestimate the power of our influence on the young, positively or negatively. I wonder whether James Dobson's father ever dreamed that, by majoring on being an exceptional father, his son would be used of God to head up a ministry with positive global impact, a ministry called Focus on the Family.

Similarly, Ronald Reagan, the extremely popular former president of the United States, frequently referred to the enormous influence his godly mother had on his life. He often quoted Scripture verses from her well-marked and worn Bible, which he used and treasured.

As a Christian, being involved in training children on a regular basis is one of the most demanding, self-sacrificing, time-consuming ministries of all. It requires great discipline, especially if it's related to parenthood, but not exclusively so. It has potential for heartbreak and disappointment. It represents great challenges and responsibilities. At the same time, the opportunities are limitless and it can become one of the most deeply rewarding and fulfilling assignments in the world.

The challenge and responsibility of the discipler is

that the little disciples will have the greatest opportunity of frequently being exposed to the character weaknesses of the discipler. The opportunity is that if the discipler is real (the most Christlike), the potential for the little disciples to become *real*, is unsurpassed.

Pursuing God with intensity is contagious. When the children see that we are genuinely ruined for the ordinary, that becomes a strong incentive for them to follow suit. My husband, Jim, and I have proved it with our children and grandchildren.

Another major factor in effectively mentoring young disciples is to involve the children with us, whenever possible, in our hot pursuit of knowing God in order to make Him known. That takes time, prayer, creativity, enthusiasm, consistency, surprises and deep commitment.

We must understand that children are far more influenced by what a hot pursuit after the knowledge of God's character and ways has done to make us *real* than all the talk about what we want and think they should become. "Observe and *obey* all these words which I command you, that it may go well with you and your children after you forever, when *you do* what

3

is good and right in the sight of the Lord your God" (Deuteronomy 12:28, emphasis mine).

We should also reiterate to children that the privilege of pursuing and serving God is always higher than the price. If we say and show that we're excited about pursuing God because we're convinced that He is the most exciting Being in the universe—and then in turn involve them in the same pursuit—we would wonder why they would want to choose anything else or less. Usually, they don't!

I was delighted to recently endorse a unique and fascinating book by Esther S. Ilnisky entitled, *Let The Children Pray*. It's fabulous and profound. It's all about how God has been and is using children as vital, history-shaping intercessors related to global projects. In their own words, they say with unabashed enthusiasm, "We're not just cute! We're mighty prayer warriors. Y-Yes!" A three-and-a-half-year-old child said, "Praying is more fun than toys."

Esther has been used of God to write her book with authority because she has been encouraging and teaching young children to become powerful intercessors for many years and has seen incredible results. She and her team headed up the children's section of the International Prayer track at the A.D. 2000 and Beyond Movement Global consultation on World Evangelism in Seoul, Korea. The global impact of the Holy Spirit's power on and through those forty children cannot be measured.

But the main point I want to make here is that Esther was forever ruined for the ordinary from the time she was a child of three, when she frequently partnered in prayer with her intercessor mother to pray for global needs. Read and enjoy her story.

Karl Barth, a Swiss theologian of the early 20th century, once said that Christians with God's heart for the world pray with the Bible in one hand and a newspaper in the other. In that case, my mother certainly knew God's heart. Daily, she could be found in her bedroom-turned-prayer room/battle station amid piles of magazines, maps, pictures and newspapers, petitioning God for, well, everything.

From the time I was three years old, we "prayed global" together. I remember crawling all over those prayer requests strewn on the floor, absorbing her prayers. When my four older siblings were off to their school, I was in mine, a school of prayer, with my teacher/mentor, my mother. A little lady and her little girl, fondly called "Estherbaby." Two giant prayer warriors.

As Mother's exquisite voice cried out for worlds beyond her human reach, my little voice would cry out, too. Her joyful praise was contagious. Her dancing heart rejoiced in what her spirit's perfect vision saw in response to her passionate petitions. My little feet then would dance about. She was my example. I did everything she did. Best of all she made me feel like a very important partner.

Mother led our church's Ladies Prayer Meeting. Every Wednesday without fail, she'd whisk me, just a preschooler, off with her to that all-important meeting. Etched on my heart forever are those numberless hours in the presence of faithful prayer warrior women who, while in the process of changing the world, were shaping my future.

Wow! What an impressive testimony! And what monumental results!

AVOIDING ALL HYPOCRISY

"O.K.," you say. "It makes sense that involving children in our exciting pursuit of God highly motivates them to do the same, but tell me more about how it works."

I'd be delighted.

Start the process as early in their lives as possible. And remember, it only works to the degree that we are committed to treating like the plague all inconsistency, phoneyism and hypocrisy in ourselves.[1]

Paul was so "for real" that he could say to the Corinthian believers that he had sent Timothy, whom he had discipled, to visit them and remind them about the truths Paul had taught them and consistently lived as a way of life (see 1 Corinthians 4:17). No one would know Paul's character better than Timothy. And no one will know our character better than the ones who are around us much of the time.

If a major part of our life's goal is to be submitted to the Holy Spirit to make us more Christlike, then we should determine never to willfully say or do anything that would distort God's character to the children we're trying to influence. If we fail, we should quickly admit it, ask for their forgiveness and then explain what we should have said or done. "He who covers his sins will not prosper, but whoever confesses and forsakes them will have mercy" (Proverbs 28:13). Then, we need to point out what aspect of God's character we didn't live up to and explain what God is really like.

So many adults have a difficult time relating to God as their Father—probably because the characteristics of real fatherhood were missing in their earthly fathers, or worse yet, they never knew who their father was. Tragically, that's the story of far too many. That's why I have given so much space in this book to how godly, single mothers can be used of God to raise children who are outstanding young adults. Unquestionably, the same can be said of godly, single fathers.

Let's take the characteristics of dependability and faithfulness. Did you, dear reader, have a dad who always followed through when he said he would do something? Fortunately, both of my parents did. Therefore, faith in God's ability and commitment to fulfill His promises from His Word to me has never been a struggle. But for millions whose story is the exact opposite, I can understand the difficulty in simply believing God will come through in His time and way, and that any delays are always for our good. They simply have nothing to relate to on the human level. That is so sad. But, as chapter six proves, God and the single parent can more than make up for that deficit.

The bottom line is this: adults who are discipling children subconsciously send signals to the children, by their adult characteristics, about what God's characteristics are. Adults are the authority figures closest to the children. And children know that the ultimate authority figure is God, so they automatically link these authorities together and act and react accordingly. That's why it's so important to always acknowledge to children, and to repent of, anything we do that distorts God's character to them.

I have asked my nineteen-year-old grandson, Matthew Dawson, to share some of the strongest influences in his life, regarding the choices he has made to be radically ruined for the ordinary. He has recently attended two different overseas training schools, both of which are three months in duration, and both are followed by two months of evangelistic outreach. This training is with Youth With A Mission (also called YWAM), which is an interdenominational missionary organization ministering in 126 nations. Matthew is presently on staff in YWAM, overseas. Here's his testimony.

First and foremost, it has been the unconditional love from my parents that has made a lasting impression on my life about God's unconditional love for me. There are two main things my father has done throughout my childhood that have helped me so much to see the true character of God. The first is that he always quickly forgave me and expressed love to me, whatever my offense. He did punish me when he needed to, but he made me understand that his punishment was an act of loving discipline and not of anger. The second thing Dad did was to always make it clear by his actions that he loved me and my family more than he loved himself. He always prioritized our interests above his own. My mother has greatly helped me to understand intimacy with Jesus and His caring, compassionate love to me by always expressing understanding of my emotions and empathizing with them with gentleness and affection.

Another area of major influence in my life has been observing that the adults who lived the most fulfilling, exciting lives were the ones who were living the most abandoned lives of obedience and faith toward God. From the very moment the thought penetrated my brain that walking with God would be intense, adventurous and radical, it has had tremendous appeal.

I've watched, and heard stories from the lives of my grandparents, Jim and Joy Dawson, who have repeatedly taken huge steps of obedience and faith in relation to God's directions, and have seen and heard how the Lord has always come through in His absolute faithfulness and has blessed them beyond anything they could have thought. It's been the same with my parents and other missionary families I have known. It became quite simple to me as a young boy that when you say "Yes," to God in all things, you then watch Him bless your socks off! But not without testings.

It wasn't the financial blessings that meant so much to me, however. It was the peace and joy that

11

I saw so clearly in God-fearing families like mine and others, that I noticed was absent in other families, that made me so desire a close relationship with God.

God has used my oldest brother, David, in a huge way to demonstrate God's faithfulness to me. I have closely observed that, ever since the day David surrendered his will to the Lord, His hand of blessing has been strongly upon him. But what I've craved the most is the humility, peace and joy that is as evident as the color of his shirt. It comes from his trust in the Lord, regardless of the circumstances.

However, I guess I gave my life completely over to the Lord because of one major reason. I found out who He really is. I can't see any reason why people in this world wouldn't surrender their lives to Jesus Christ other than that, sadly, they don't understand what He's really like. My point is that my family and other spiritual leaders portrayed to me, as accurately as humanly possible, the real character of God. And nothing has been more devastating to the enemy's plan for my life than being the recipient of God's unconditional love through God-fearing people.

My comment to that sold-out-to-the-Lord teenager's testimony is: "To whom much has been given," Jesus said, "much will be required" (see Luke 12:48). It has been so in my life and will be so in my precious grandson's life. We should never be envious or jealous of those who have had the enormous privilege of a strong Christian heritage. Rather, we should pray that they will be clothed with the fear of the Lord and be given the supernatural humility and grace needed to discharge the more-than-average accountabilities and responsibilities that will inevitably be given them by our God of absolute justice.

HOW ARE WE INVESTING?

Now let's observe the different ways by which two prominent leaders in the Bible approached their accountability and responsibility toward their respective succeeding generations.

King Hezekiah had been mightily used of God to spearhead and lead a time of genuine reformation and revival among God's people during his twenty-nine years of leadership.

After this same king had been miraculously healed by God from near death and fifteen more years had been added to his life, God declared to him, through Isaiah the prophet, that two things would take place. The first was that God would deliver and defend Hezekiah and the city in which he lived from his enemy, the king of Assyria. The second was that, in the future days, the accumulation of all Hezekiah's valuable possessions would be confiscated and taken away to Babylon, and some of his own sons would be taken captive in that city by enemy forces.

King Hezekiah's reaction to these grave, prophetic announcements was surprisingly apathetic, considering how mightily he had seen God work during his time of leadership. It also discloses the total lack of spiritual ambition for the generation that would follow him. "So Hezekiah said to Isaiah, 'The word of the Lord which you have spoken is good!' For he said, 'Will there not be peace and truth at least in my days?'" (2 Kings 20:19).

Hezekiah's lack of concern, and subsequent lack of spiritual preparation for the next generation, no doubt contributed to the fact that his son and successor, Manassah, manifested a blatant disregard for the things of God and led the nation accordingly. May Hezekiah's failure at this point in his life serve as a strong reminder to us *not* to follow his example.

Our young people of today are tomorrow's leaders. Let us take seriously our accountability to God and responsibility to the young to consistently influence them in such a way that they will be ready to lead their generation in the fear of the Lord and the ways of God.

In Psalm 22:30–31, King David could confidently state that "Our children too shall serve him, for they shall hear from us about the wonders of the Lord; generations yet unborn shall hear of all the miracles he did for us" (TLB). This powerful testimony came from a prominent spiritual leader who had not only been greatly used of God in his lifetime, but who repeatedly manifested strong spiritual ambition for the generation following him.

Listen to David's strong exhortation to his son Solomon, who succeeded him. "Know the God of your father, and serve Him with a loyal heart and with a willing mind; for the Lord searches all hearts and understands all the intent of the thoughts. If you seek Him, He will be found by you; but if you forsake Him,

He will cast you off forever" (1 Chronicles 28:9). This is followed by equally strong encouragement in verse 10, "Consider now, for the Lord has chosen you to build a house for the sanctuary; be strong and do it."

David then showed the extent of his commitment to future generations by not only giving generously out of his personal financial resources, but urging others to do the same. "Moreover, because I have set my affection on the house of my God, I have given to the house of my God, over and above all that I have prepared for the holy house, my own special treasure of gold and silver. I know also, my God, that You test the heart and have pleasure in uprightness. As for me, in the uprightness of my heart I have willingly offered all these things; and now with joy I have seen Your people, who are present here to offer willingly to You" (1 Chronicles 29:3, 17).

However, David understood that the most power-ful and most lasting way to ensure that those who fol-lowed him fulfilled their God-ordained destinies was through fervent intercession for them to live a life of obedience to God. Listen to his prayer, " . . . fix their heart toward You. And give my son Solomon a loyal heart to keep Your commandments and Your testimonies and Your statutes, to do all these things, and to build the temple for which I have made provision" (1 Chronicles 29:18b, 19).

Now, let us examine our lives in the light of what we have seen in the lives of these two spiritual leaders. Let us assess, in all honesty, how we match up in relation to our involvement with future generations. Are we teaching them and encouraging them, giving our resources to help them, and praying fervently and frequently for them? If we are, we are already experiencing a real measure of fulfillment. If we are not, then there's no better time than right now to determine to re-prioritize our involvement, resources and prayer lives on their behalf.

If you don't know how to start, God does. Ask Him. It's never too late. Everyone with a sincere desire to be linked with the younger generations will discover that God not only knows who to link them with, but how to bring about the encounter. If you are in this category, dear reader, you are in for a thrilling, rewarding investment. Here's a classic example.

I have a dear intercessor friend, Emma Fitzhugh, who is now eighty-three years young. She had belonged for many years to a vital, suburban church where she had numbers of friends and was loved and respected. A few years ago her pastor announced to his congregation a need for someone to leave his church and become a permanent, active, committed member of a small, African American church in the inner city. He asked the people to see what God would say to them as they individually sought Him.

I wasn't surprised when I learned that it was my friend Emma to whom God gave the missionary call. The point of this story is that at age eighty she found that her main mission field is young people! She loves them dearly and they gravitate to her like bees to honey. She is very young at heart and vibrant in spirit. There's something about this veteran in the faith that generates the kind of genuine stability, warmth and wisdom this disillusioned, orphaned generation desperately needs and yearns to find.

Emma never has a spare or a dull moment. She doesn't know the meaning of boredom or discontent. She lives for the Lord and for others and is heavily investing her life in the succeeding generations. I salute her!

MENTORING GOD'S PRIORITIES

We desperately need to mentor God's priorities to the young disciples who are within the scope of our influence. Ours and their priorities determine our mutual destinies. So our choices to live by God's priorities become serious business. Destinies are at stake.

1) The Word of God

As adults, we need to take time studying God's character from His Word in order to understand Him so that we know how *not* to distort God's character to the impressionable children we're influencing. And there are no crash courses or shortcuts for that rewarding pursuit.

Words are inadequate for me to describe the inestimable benefit I have derived from working with a large alphabetized notebook alongside my Bible during my daily devotional time with the Lord.

When I read from the Scriptures an attribute of God's character, say for instance, His holiness, I turn to the pages in my notebook allotted to the letter "H" and write THE HOLINESS OF GOD as the heading. Then I write out the entire verse surrounding the word *holiness*. Subsequently, I meditate on what that verse says about this part of God's character, asking and believing the Holy Spirit to give me revelation. At the same time, with the same method, I study the ways of God or the principles by which He works. For example, when I read a verse about obedience, or waiting on God, or the fear of the Lord, I turn to the pages allotted to O, W, or F, make the appropriate subject headings at the top of the page and then write out the verses, etc.

This way, I have built up my own personal concordance on the character and ways of God from thousands of Bible verses and it has become the basis of all my teachings and writings. This invaluable training in the school of the Holy Spirit from the Word of God has been and still is absolutely priceless to me. In

Jeremiah 9:23–24, God makes it abundantly clear as to the rating He gives to understanding His character. It's a top priority! He states that the things that impress people the most, earthly knowledge, positions of authority and material wealth, are totally unimpressive to Him. God is only impressed with those who have taken the time to understand and know Him (see verse 24). This school of learning is in His Word, the Bible.

I have asked my son, John, founder and president of the International Reconciliation Coalition, to share his testimony in regard to his using this same method of Bible study.

At the age of nineteen, far from home during my first experience of missionary training, desperate for reassurance, I remembered Mom's method of Bible study.

I went to a department store in Lausanne, Switzerland, purchased a notebook, and alphabetized it with little tabs. My first subjects were survival needs—overcoming temptation, pride and humility, and, of course, God's provision because I was beginning a life of faith.

21

Even with the masterful lectures from teachers such as Brother Andrew and Corrie ten Boom, the highlight of each day became the process of receiving revelation on the Scriptures from the Holy Spirit and carefully recording it in the appropriate page in my personal concordance.

It's still the highlight of my day. Having passed 50, I look back over 30 years of fruitful ministry, much of which flows from the foundational experience of studying the character and ways of God in this way.

The original notebook is dog-eared and preserved beneath a new cover. It is the basis for my teaching. I find that it is those Scriptures, first recorded as a teenager, that flow easily from memory when I'm preaching. They have been woven into the very fabric of my being. When I'm writing a book, they spring to mind; when I'm facing a crisis, they become the revelation of God's own heart to me, the comfort of the Living Word. My oldest son is an urban missionary, frequently involved in pastoring. He has a notebook like his grandmother's and mine. I have confidence in his future.

Another key to effective discipling is to let the children know and see that time with God in His Word is a daily priority in your life. The following verses from Psalm 119 affirm that priority. "The law of Your mouth is better to me than thousands of coins of gold and silver" (Psalm 119:72). "My hands also I will lift up to Your commandments, which I love, and I will meditate on Your statutes" (Psalm 119:48). "Your testimonies also are my delight and my counselors" (Psalm 119:24).

On one occasion, when my eldest grandson was four years of age and staying with me, I gently but firmly told him that both of us needed to be quiet for a while because I was going to read my Bible and listen to what God had to say to me. David immediately saw my little *Daily Light* book, which is nothing but scriptures related to the same theme, put together for both the morning and evening of the same day. He opened it and took off "preaching" a most unique "message" of truths he had learned. Out came salient, basic truths about the Gospel message mixed in with a four-year-old's vivid imagination—fascinating to say the least. I captured the moment by making full notes, strongly encouraged him, and then went on with my Bible reading while he played with his toys near me. (David, now twenty-six, has been in full-time ministry for nine years.)

Undoubtedly, my passionate love for the Bible started from my earliest childhood when I saw that the Bible was by far the most important book in my Dad's personal life—and he had an enormous library. God's Word was so important to him that, every week-night after dinner, he read to his five children from an interesting version especially suitable for children. (He actually wore out one copy through constant use and had to have a replacement!) Dad then asked us questions about what we had heard and learned. I was never bored. God's Word fascinated me then and increasingly does so now.

If we want the children we're discipling to be worshippers, intercessors, lovers of God's Word, sharers of their faith in the Lord, givers, and those who hear and obey God's voice, we'll need to make these things priorities in our own lives on a daily basis and then ask God to show us ways to involve them in those pursuits whenever expedient.

2) Intercession (praying for others)

Regular times of family worship, which include reading about and explaining the character and ways of God from His Word, followed by involving the children in praying for other people's needs, is a great way to do this. "And these words which I command you today shall be in your heart. You shall teach them diligently to your children, and shall talk of them when you sit in your house, when you walk by the way, when you lie down, and when you rise up. You shall bind them as a sign on your hand, and they shall be as frontlets between your eyes" (Deuteronomy 6:6–8). With our children, we varied these times by reading about or sharing vital, interesting stories about Divine intervention in times of human need. And we learned to make sure that nothing was allowed to divert us during these times, like making sure the phone was temporarily taken off the hook.

I can imagine a mother with young children under school age thinking, "C'mon, get real. How on earth can I be involved in intercession when I never have a spare minute?" My answer is, "We make time for what we really want to do."

A young mother with three children and due to have her fourth child any day, heard me teaching on our responsibility as individuals to be praying for the nations and how to do it effectively. God's Word says, "My house shall be called a house of prayer for all nations" (Isaiah 56:7b).[2] When her baby was born, she figured out that the only time in the day that she could fulfill that injunction was when she was breast-feeding her baby. She took that time to pray for different aspects of the Body of Christ in the particular nation to which God directed her that day.

During the course of each day, that determined mother was being obedient to one of God's priorities. This probably contributed to the fact that she and her husband and four children, now adults, have been effectively involved in an international missionary organization for many years. World vision starts with intercession for every nation, on a systematic basis.[3]

Years ago, when my dear friend, Shelagh McAlpine, and I met every Thursday afternoon to pray for the nations, Shelagh's fourth child, John, was just a baby. When he was at the crawling stage, in order to keep him amused, at times I would crawl around the floor on my hands and knees with him on my back. I can remember doing this while Shelagh and I were alternately praying fervently for the nation of China. Today we are seeing answers to those many prayers.

But what about the days when the children are "impossible" and you feel about as spiritual as a croaking frog? Perhaps you started coaxing them lovingly to quit the fighting and the racket, then you resorted to yelling at them out of exasperation and finally you said they would pay for their rambunctious behavior when their dad came home from work. They cooperated as much as if you'd spoken to a bunch of cockroaches.

Having worship music fill the house, combined with involving the precious little brats in a fun project with yourself during this kind of scenario is a powerful combination. Recently, a distraught mother of three young children e-mailed our daughter Jill and asked her for some advice while trying to keep her sanity on "one of those days."

Jill's response included telling the mother to play a praise-and-worship CD in her house and to pray fervently for God's help and intervention. Then she suggested putting the children in front of a mirror and having all of them make funny faces and laugh with and at each other. I thought that was great advice and told her so.

In addition, I would suggest that spiritual warfare be done by participating in the praise and commanding the forces of darkness to cease operations in the all powerful name of the Lord Jesus Christ, quoting in faith, "Resist the devil and he will flee from you" (James 4:7), or other related scriptures.

3) Listening and obeying

Our children learned to hear God's voice as a most natural occurrence when they were very young. This was done through teaching them to listen to God's directions, whether during family times of praying for other's needs or seeking God together for guidance in family related matters. As soon as children can talk, we can teach them to listen to God and talk to Him.[4] He promises to respond. Psalm 32:8 says, "I will instruct you and teach you in the way you should go; I will guide you with My eye." And Jesus says in John 10:27, "My sheep hear My voice, and I know them, and they follow Me."

It was during our regular and frequent times of intercession together as a family that our children primarily learned to hear God's voice. We taught them that praying for the needs of others always preceded praying for any of our personal or family needs. Many times, during or straight after the evening meal together, we would share the needs of others, mostly from information we read in interdenominational and international mission-related magazines.

During our intercession times the children knew that whoever God chose to put His thoughts into their minds first, could be the first one to pray. There was never a planned order. On one occasion when our daughter Jill was five years old, the Holy Spirit moved on her in this way first, and she was interceding for someone else's need when suddenly she said, "Oh, I feel faint." Her little face went white and she started to fall back on her heels. We were all kneeling. Instantly, I sensed this was a demonic attack, moved over to her, and forcefully resisted the enemy in the all-powerful name of the Lord Jesus Christ. She recovered quickly and I said, "We won't give the devil any more attention by allowing him to disrupt this prayer time, so go right on praying, darling." And she did.

Satanic forces are well aware of the potential of children becoming vital disciples of Christ and having world vision when they are involved in intercession for peoples and nations as a way of life. Praying that way produces the kind of environment that is likely to result in world changers under the power of the Holy Spirit. In the incident involving Jill, which I shared above, the enemy found out that we were unimpressed with his tactics by trying to hinder the fulfillment of those purposes. We were never interrupted like that again.

Growing up in an environment of waiting on God in silence, expecting to hear God's voice, in any one of the twenty-five ways He speaks,[4] speaking aloud the impressions He gives and in time seeing or hearing the results, will greatly help to keep a family pursuing God together, especially when experienced in an atmosphere of wonderment, excitement and worship because of who God is. "For since the beginning of the world men have not heard nor perceived by the ear, nor has the eye seen any God besides You, who acts for the one who waits for Him" (Isaiah 64:4).

This truth was dramatically illustrated to our children when John was around ten years of age and Jill was six. Each year, Jim and I sought God diligently for directions as to where we would spend our summer holiday time with our children. That year, to our surprise, there was nothing but silence from headquarters Heaven every time we inquired. We explained this to the children, encouraging them to wait on God with us, trusting in His faithfulness.

The nearer it came to vacation time, the more awkward it became for our children because their friends kept asking John and Jill where they were going. All they could say was, "We don't know yet." Everyone was aware of the need for advance reservations at the campgrounds at that time of the year in New Zealand, where we lived. And we sure loved camping holidays.

On the Sunday morning, one week before the holidays, just as we were leaving our church service, I heard the Holy Spirit speak into my spirit, "Today I am going to tell you where to go for your holiday." I shared this breakthrough with the family when we all got in our car. Expectancy and excitement, as well as relief, were running high. We had just sat down for our midday meal when the Holy Spirit impressed these words upon my mind, "Phone the campground [specifically naming one of the ones that we would have wanted to go to] and make your reservation." I acted promptly, and asked for the very best camping site right by the beachfront row. It was a fairly large campground, but with relatively few campsites along the small beachfront. I figured that, because of God's sheer goodness and unparalleled greatness, I would ask for the best, remembering too, the rewards of waiting on God from Isaiah 64:4.

The woman on the end of the phone said, "There's not a campsite available anywhere, and the few choice sites you're inquiring about have all been booked a year in advance." I replied, "Yes, I totally understand that is how it works, but I am still making the same request." And I held my breath. Suddenly she said, "Hold on a minute." I kept thanking God by faith for His provision. When she returned she said, "I have just this second been informed that one of the sites you are describing has been cancelled while you were talking to me; I guess you may as well have it as anyone else. It's yours."

You can imagine the hoopla that reverberated throughout our house. But that was nothing compared to the wonder and excitement we all experienced when we arrived. Our allocated site was right beside a shady tree in the exact location for which I had asked. And on the next site to us was a lovely family with a boy John's age and a little girl Jill's age. They had a rowboat which the boys, in particular, enjoyed every day. It was the perfect set-up in every way and we had a fabulous vacation. God is so faithful and incredibly personal.

Our children learned that, "They shall not be ashamed who wait for Me" (Isaiah 49:23). They were learning to understand the character and ways of God while being shaped to live extraordinarily. There were other such times when we experienced the "impossible with man" breakthroughs for vacation camping times by moving only at God's directions and timetable. Each occasion was used by God to convey to our children that living according to God's ways is where the real action and fulfillment is.

4) Sharing our faith naturally

Our goal should not only be to know God but to make Him known. After all, Jesus said "Follow Me, and I will make you fishers of men" (Matthew 4:19). In other words, the purpose of passionately pursuing God is that we might influence others to passionately pursue Him.[5] Even in fulfilling the priority of evangelism, we need to heed a warning. We should never try to win the world for Christ at the expense of losing our own children to the devil. "Be diligent to know the state of your flocks and attend to your herds" (Proverbs 27:23). Our "flocks" involve more than being responsible to giving adequate attention to the means by which income is generated. Our flocks can mean our little (or big) ones, as well.

Satan's main ministry is to distort the character of God to everyone, Christian and non-Christian. Neglecting our children will help to do just that in a hurry. The more children observe in us that witnessing for Christ is a normal, natural, joyous part of our everyday lives and not an event, the more likely they will choose to live unselfishly and want to obey the Great Commission in Matthew 28:19–20: "Go therefore and make disciples of all the nations, baptizing them in the name of the Father and of the Son and of the Holy Spirit, teaching them to observe all things that I have commanded you; and lo, I am with you always, even to the end of the age."

In both my parents' lives, witnessing for Christ and meeting human needs was about as natural and normal as eating and sleeping. It deeply impacted my life. But we five children were not neglected in their zeal to win the lost to Christ. How very grateful and accordingly responsible I am to mentor others in the same way.

An intimate relationship with God is experienced by making what is important to God, important to us. And the importance and value that Jesus placed upon little children was so high that He said it would be better for a person to put a millstone around his or her neck and get drowned in the sea than to offend any one of them (see Matthew 18:6). If in our intense pursuit of God's manifest presence and glory we neglect the children for whom we're responsible, God is not only unimpressed, He's grieved.

My husband, Jim, and I were involved in numerous forms of evangelism when our children were small and growing up. We either took turns in staying home with them (even in their teens) while the other one was out in ministry, or we had the children with us, or the personal evangelism was going on in our home, or a family friend with whom the children were familiar and secure stayed with them.

By God's grace and mercy, our children responded to the call of God to be missionaries in their teens and have remained as such for all these subsequent years. Their children are now choosing the same lifestyle.

This does not mean that as parents and grand-parents we have been exempt from times of heartache and intensive spiritual warfare in order for those choices to be made. The enemy targets those he thinks have the greatest potential to be a threat to his cause.

If you, dear reader, are going through times of heartache, disappointment and perplexity over those for whom you have invested much in prayer, loving service, friendship and training, be encouraged, you are not alone. I don't know of anyone in this category who has escaped these testing times in one way or another.

I have often observed that children who have equally been influenced by a heritage and environment of love, righteousness and security, can make totally different choices in relation to spiritual things. This is understandably perplexing, but God has a solution for that situation.

We can take comfort and encouragement from the fact that Jesus used the parable of the shepherd who wasn't as concerned for the sheep that were in the fold as He was for the one that was lost. He went to great lengths to find it and rescue it (see Matthew 18:12–24). Hang in there and believe that light overcomes darkness. Love is stronger than hate. Forgiveness diffuses hostility. And God's power, purposes and plans for those for whom you are burdened, make Satan's efforts toward them look pale and puny. So much "Greater is he that is in you, than he that is in the world" (1 John 4:4, KJV).

5) Giving

Why is learning to give, as a way of life, so important? Because if we only have input into our lives, and no output, we get stagnant. As in the case of the sea in Israel, which has no outlet, stagnation produces death—that's why it's called the Dead Sea.

When the same principle is applied to our bodies, our intestines get blocked. If that's not corrected, we'll die too. Lack of giving out to others from the blessings we have received ultimately ends in some form of death. Jesus said that when we give our lives away to Him on behalf of others, we will gain life (see Matthew 16:25). Conversely, when we save our lives by living selfishly, we will lose them. That's one of God's spiritual laws. But there's another more important reason.

We need to learn to be radical givers in order to become more like the ultimate Giver, God Himself. His unfathomable love was demonstrated by the extent of the incredible lengths He went to in order to give His most priceless gift, His only begotten Son, the Lord Jesus Christ, who became sin for all mankind. Mind-boggling and totally awesome in its concepts and implications.

A plain caterpillar remains in a drab-looking chrysalis, and then after a considerable struggle, emerges and is released as a beautiful, liberated butterfly. This is an analogy of how God works to produce the ultimate purpose in our lives of conforming us all to the likeness of His Son (see Romans 8:29). And one of the ways for that metamorphosis to take place is to teach us how to be radical, delighted givers—of ourselves and anything we possess—at any time to anyone, anywhere, in obedience to God's clear directions.

First Timothy 6:10 says that "the *love* of money is a root of all kinds of evil" [emphasis mine]. Therefore, it makes sense to me that we need to be freed from that evil root. Having God's perspective on money is the easiest way I know to achieve that freedom.

I cannot adequately express to you the fabulous freedom that came many years ago when God revealed directly to me that money is only paper that God uses to test our obedience to Him. That means we will give it away, receive it or spend it, with abandoned joy according to His instructions and sovereign purposes. God owns everything, according to Psalm 50:12: "The world is mine, and all that is in it," (NIV) and we've already established that He is the most lavish giver. Therefore, He is neither poor nor mean. There-fore, He doesn't need anything. Therefore, lack of money has never been a problem to Him. His purpose is to get us to see His viewpoint concerning it.

Want to help shape the lives of future history makers? Demonstrate these principles to them by your lifestyle. They will catch on quickly, be fascinated by the implications and outcomes and with childlike freedom will "join the club." I'll illustrate here.

In 1972, in obedience to God's directions, the leadership of Y.W.A.M. contracted by faith to buy a castle in Hurlach, Germany for a missionary training center. We had no money. God honored our obedience and faith, and our friend, Brother Andrew (also known as "God's Smuggler"), gave us the $10,000 needed for the down payment.

When it came time for the first monthly payment, our founder and president, Loren Cunningham, asked about 1200 of us, who had come from all over the world to witness at the Munich Olympic Games, to be obedient to whatever God told us to do in regard to meeting that need. Our daughter Jill was sixteen years old at the time. She wept, because she had no money to put into the big offering basket. She so longed to be able to give.

On that day and the next two days, through a series of three remarkable incidents that could only have been explained and orchestrated by God, three different people unexpectedly gave her monetary gifts. Each time she was given a gift, which increased in amounts, she ran to the front of the large tent we were all in for the daily meetings, and gave away every penny. Her tears turned to pure joy!! Main point being, God will always give to those who *want* to give, any amount, any time, anywhere.

Today, Jill is running a home-based business (while homeschooling her teenage son, Justin) for the sole purpose of supporting twelve full-time national volunteers who are ministering to the poor and needy with Y.W.A.M. in India. Every penny earned goes to their support, while Jill and her husband, John Bills, live entirely by faith, as all Y.W.A.Mers do. Jill still experiences and exudes the same delighted joy of lavish giving that she did as a young teenager. God loves it, and so do I. By the way, both of Jill's children have participated in numbers of missions trips in foreign countries, and her daughter, Jenny, is a full-time missionary in Y.W.A.M.

6) Worship

Everything we do should start with worship, be punctuated with worship and end with worship, according to Psalm 34:1: "I will bless the Lord at all times; His praise shall continually be in my mouth." When children are surrounded by praising adults and praise and worship music, it produces the ultimate positive environment in which they can function. And there's nothing that defeats Satan's plans in any situation more than an atmosphere that is charged with praise and worship to God, coming from hearts and lives who are delighting themselves in Him.

When we make this a way of life, not just something we do as part of the liturgy when we go to church, the children around us pick up the signals (consciously or subconsciously) that God is in charge, and regardless of the circumstances, everything is going to be O.K. What an incredible security that gives them—and us!

Our son, John, is a wonderful example of this as a parent. It makes no difference whether the occasion is a family celebration, or we're just together, or there's a challenging family problem, his response is delightfully predictable: "Let's worship the Lord together." He leads by singing and playing worship songs on his guitar and whoever is around joins in. Little wonder that I've observed his grown sons doing exactly the same thing, while their little sister, Rachael, dances around with joyous abandonment. Tremendous unity and peace descends upon any group when Jesus is given center stage through praise and worship.

PEER PRESSURE

P eers are an enormous influence, for good or for bad, on the young ones we're discipling. Being accepted by their friends is of major importance, and children will go to almost any lengths to have this desire fulfilled. Rugged individuality seldom manifests itself with children in a group situation.

With this in mind, how important is it that the children we're trying to raise to be history shapers, have their closest friendships with children from homes that have the highest Biblical standards of living? The obvious answer is, it is of major importance.

So where do we usually find those children who will have this inevitable influence on our kids? Most likely at the vital church fellowship of God's choice for us and them. He knows which and where that church is, and will direct us to it as we seek Him with an open mind and a willing heart to obey Him. After all, God is far more concerned than we are that our children be exposed to the right influences rather than the wrong ones.

The crunch comes here when we realize again that our greatest influence on the children we're discipling comes from our own lives. That means we ourselves need to be involved with the vital church of God's choosing, on a regular basis. When the children see that it's important enough for us as adults to make a priority of integrating our lives with regular worship and servanthood at that particular church, and that we do it joyously, their normal response will be to do the same within the programs provided for them.

Loneliness is one of the hardest things for children to handle. They're inevitably going to gravitate to other kids who will accept them. If they're not regularly exposed to those from the families with the highest Biblical standards, they'll gravitate to those who don't have those standards. And that's when negative peer pressure most often sets in, with damaging results.

We also need to be sensitive and obedient to the promptings of the Holy Spirit in regard to warnings He may give us concerning the children we are discipling. It shouldn't depend on whether or not we have any or little understanding as to the purpose of the Divine constraint or restraint in our spirits as He warns us.

When our son, John, was about twelve years old, he was friendly with a certain boy in our neighborhood—a nice, normal-looking kid. I had no personal dislike for this particular boy, nor any known reason why God had placed such a strong impression upon me that we were to forbid John to continue to go to this boy's home. We explained this to John and trusted him to obey our counsel and to trust God with us for the reasons, which he did. It wasn't until recently, when I shared this incident with John, that he remembered that the boy was involved in thievery.

It's of major importance that the children get involved as early as possible in reaching out to and serving others in need. As we set the example of service for them, we make it easier for them to follow our lead, both in the home and in the church environment.

I was interested to read in the *Pentecostal Evangel* (June 24, 2001), in the "News Digest" section, the opening article by Katy Attananasi, "Prison Chaplain Hooked on Ministry." The author writes:

Kathy Radke is quick to tell people, teasingly, she has been in and out of jail since she was 13 years old. As a teen, she and other members from her youth group held Sunday afternoon services in an area jail. She's been involved in prison ministry ever since. In addition to her responsibilities as an associate minister at Westbank Cathedral (Assemblies of God) in Marrero, LA., Radke serves as the Protestant chaplain at the Jefferson Parish Correctional Center and at Riverdale Juvenile Detention Center. Her responsibilities include coordinating worship services and Bible studies as well as scheduling volunteers and area churches to minister at the centers.

(Reprinted by permission of *Pentecostal Evangel* magazine.)

It is very significant to me that Kathy's vital life's ministry started at the early age of thirteen by being involved in reaching out to needy people, in this case, prisoners. And the opportunity came from her home church group.

When our children were young, Jim and I were involved in one of the most rewarding ministry assignments of our lives—regularly visiting prisoners. We asked the prison officials to allow us to visit the inmates who had the least visitors. Some had none. Some of them, like child molesters, turned out to be those who were despised by their families and the other prisoners.

After proving our genuine God-given love for these kinds of men, over time, they accepted us as close friends. By God's grace we were able to lead some of them to the Lord, and when they were finally released after years of being incarcerated, one of them came to stay in our home until we were able to help him find employment and housing. Others came to our home as visitors. We regularly kept in touch with them. They were our friends.

A few years after we left New Zealand in 1971 and came to the U.S. as missionaries with Youth With A Mission, we were awakened in the middle of the night by a phone call from an ex-prisoner telling us how well he was doing in every way. Well worth the broken sleep!

The point of this story is that our children were deeply impacted by our lifestyle in this regard. They were involved in the joy and fulfillment of seeing the dregs of society transformed by the grace of God into followers of the Lord Jesus. It helped to lay the foundation for their choosing for themselves to make reaching out to needy people a way of life.

For several years, our daughter Jill and son-in-law, John Bills, had an effective ministry to refugees in the camps in Thailand, and since then to people with AIDS. In the early days of the epidemic, when there was so much concern about the contagious nature of the disease, they even took one AIDS patient into their home for the remaining four months of his life. They lovingly cared for him like a family member until he went to be with the Lord.

You may be wondering why we were not afraid to bring an ex-child molester into our home when our children were small. Or why John and Jill Bills were unafraid to have a man with an advanced case of AIDS living with them for months, especially at a time when his disease was uncontrollable. The answer in both cases is the same. We, and they, were compelled and directed by our God of unfathomable love, who graced us with His mind and His heart to obey His injunctions from His Word, to be involved with the poor and needy. And we proved the Bible truth that "Perfect love casts out fear." While Jim and I were led by God to welcome newly converted former prisoners into our home, it doesn't mean that is necessarily God's plan for everyone with small children. His plan for one family may not be the wisest plan for another.

Short-term mission trips are a wonderful way to fulfill the goal of serving the needy. I've been so impressed with the powerful spiritual impact that exposure to other races and cultures for the purpose of ministering to their needs has on children who have been on these trips. Missionary organizations and missionary-minded churches provide the organized opportunities. It's a sure way of speeding up the process of raising world changers. I challenge you, dear reader, to get involved yourself and to encourage the children you're discipling to do the same. Youth With A Mission has a wonderful ministry called "King's Kids," which fulfills these goals (see the appendix for an address). Teen Mania is another excellent organization with the same goals.

Being sold out to God and being radically real is where all the real action is. There's certainly never a dull moment. Boredom and frustration only come from doing our own thing in our way and in our time. We're not smart enough to know what's best for us. As our Creator, God is the only one who knows how to fulfill us. We certainly haven't a clue.

The most adventurous challenge we can give any child is to dare them to say and mean, "O.K. God, You're the boss. Take over. I abdicate my throne rights. You're the King. From now on, You fire the shots." They won't find that challenge hard to accept if you have taken the time to study the character of God and then take the time to teach them the same. The most logical thing in the world is to surrender our lives to the One who is infinite in wisdom and knowledge (knows the plan for our lives), unparalleled in greatness (has the power to bring it to pass), absolute in justice (we'll always get a fair deal from Him), awesome in holiness and righteousness (it will always involve 100 percent integrity), and unfathomable in love (He longs to bring the maximum blessings to us through His plan).

We do ourselves the greatest favor to run to Him and say, "All of me is Yours." His immediate response is, "O.K., then all of Me is available to you." What an incredible deal! It's unbeatable![8]

HOSPITALITY TO THE RADICALLY REAL

As a child, I was permanently impacted by the stories my father and mother shared around the dinner table about how they'd proved the reality of God in their daily lives. For example, one day the newspapers announced a severe shortage of potatoes everywhere. That night, Dad arrived home with a huge sack of potatoes, a grin from ear to ear and halfway down his back, and a story of how God had answered his prayers in an extraordinary way for this provision for his family of five children. Or to hear Mother share about her opportunities to witness for Christ to a poor neighbor with many children and an alcoholic husband, after having done the same neighbor's washing and ironing for her. And I remember the time Dad told us how he had given a hitchhiker a ride in his car that day, witnessed to him about the Lord and led him through to salvation. When Dad found out the man never owned a suit, Dad gave him one of his. Dad only had two suits, and he had them both with him, as he was on a combined business and ministry trip for a few days.

But I was forever ruined for the ordinary when I heard stories like the next one.

His name was Mr. Don Gillies, a Scottish evangelist living by faith, who frequently visited my parents' home in New Zealand. Although I had heard the story before, I was so intrigued by it, I would always say, "Please, Mr. Gillies, tell it to me one more time." And he would. Here's the story.

One day, after Mr. Gillies had left our home city of Auckland by car, he arrived in a little town (as it was then) called Warkworth. He was very hungry, but didn't have sufficient money to buy a meal. Don Gillies parked his car and walked around the few shops, asking his Heavenly Father to somehow provide him with a meal. As he was passing a small restaurant, he heard the voice of God speaking, inaudibly to his outer ear, but clearly audible to the inner ear of his spirit, "Go in there." So he did.

When he sat down and looked at the small menu, he figured that, seeing God was going to have to miraculously supply him with money for the meal, he may as well order the most substantial one available. So, that's exactly what he did. When it arrived, he bowed his head and thanked God for the food, and by faith, the money to pay for it.

No doubt all through the meal Mr. Gillies would expect someone to come into the restaurant and sit down beside or near him. Then, out of a God-ordained contact and conversation, be prompted by the Holy Spirit to pay his bill without Mr. Gillies having to say a word about his inability to do so. But it never happened that way. The meal ended, and, by faith, he went up to the cash register with the bill, wondering how (not if) his Heavenly Father would explain to him why he had received such clear direction to eat at this restaurant.

At that point, the lady behind the counter said, "My husband and I only opened this restaurant a week ago today. And we decided that the first person who came into our restaurant and bowed his or her head and gave thanks to God for the food, we would give that person the meal free of charge. You are that one." Don Gillies thanked the owner and told her how she had been used of God to meet his needs.

That story blew me away and I determined in my young heart that whatever it took, I wanted to know God and be able to hear His voice *like that*. Little would my parents or Mr. Gillies ever dream that one day I would write a book called, *Forever Ruined for the Ordinary*, sub-titled, "The Adventure of Hearing and Obeying God's Voice."

The impact that story had on my life came from my parents' having an open home, extending hospitality to many servants of the Lord, and from their encouraging my four brothers and me to sit around and listen to the stories that came from their lives.

When my husband Jim and I had our own home, we did exactly the same thing. "Open house" to God's servants was absolutely normal. In fact, we built a "prophet's chamber" onto our home, especially for that purpose.

The point of telling all this is that one of the most powerful ways of raising world changers is to regularly expose them in the home, through hospitality, to radically real people. That makes a lot of sense to me. In fact, our having a ministry of hospitality to spiritual leaders and people in full-time ministry was one of the ways God used to launch our whole family into full-time missionary service.

It was when Loren Cunningham, founder of Youth With A Mission, was staying in our home in New Zealand for several weeks, that God revealed to him (unbeknownst to me until one year later) that the Bible-teaching ministry God had given me was to be introduced to the nations. One-and-a-half years after that had taken place, God called Jim out of the business world into full-time ministry with Youth With A Mission, and our two teenage children (at that time) joined him. At the time of the writing this book, thirty-two years later, three of our grandchildren are also presently involved in Youth With A Mission.

I wonder how many destinies are waiting to be fulfilled by Christians opening their homes in hospitality to those who are fulfilling the Great Commission of Matthew 28:18–20?

Another factor in powerfully influencing children to become all that God intended them to be is the number of Sunday school teachers, youth leaders, Christian school teachers—all those, other than parents—who faithfully serve the Lord by ministering to them. Sometimes the people I've just listed are the only ones in the lives of the children who will represent the Lord Jesus to them. What a responsibility, privilege and opportunity.

My friend, lovely Karen Cunningham, has been a preschool teacher in Youth With A Mission for fourteen years. She has taught children in New Zealand, Hawaii, Hong Kong, England, Hungary, the U.S., Africa, and Singapore. Her next assignment is to be the teacher on the set of the next movie her brother, David, will be directing.

What an example Karen is of a life totally dedicated to God, where He is powerfully using her to help shape the lives of thousands of little children, in their most impressionable years, particularly in their concepts of God.

"Miss Karen," as the little ones call her, is always a favorite with them. I know. When my grandson, Matthew, was three years old and was in her class for three months, he was very fond of her. And for good reason. She is such a beautiful ambassador for Christ, representing His character and personhood so effectively. In other words, by her appearance, personality, teaching and character, she exudes the life of the One she is sold-out to and serving—her Lord. Only eternity will reveal how her life has helped to shape the lives of many future world changers.

TREATING THEM
AS FRIENDS

Our personal passion for the Lord Jesus and our devoted love, loyalty and respect for one another as parents, along with the balance of discipline and frequently expressed affection and encouragement to the children will make them feel secure. In addition, letting them see the source of our security as a way of life will give them the ultimate security. Our security comes from our submission, dependence, obedience and total trust in the Lord as we seek Him over matters large and small. It is also demonstrated in the faith-filled way we react in times of difficulty. Praise, worship and thanksgiving to God are always the "in thing" no matter what.

Our availability and approachability to young disciples is another enormous factor in their feeling secure. Conversely, repeated signals to the children that we're too busy to have quality time with them or that what they want to share is unimportant will sow seeds of insecurity and inferiority. I will not easily forget hearing international Bible teacher and author Judson Cornwall share on a teaching tape about the priority he made of being available as a father to his daughters.

When he was the pastor of a church and his children were growing up, he told them that regardless of what else he was involved in ministry-wise, if they really needed him, all they needed to do was to phone him. There were no limits placed on his availability to them.

One Sunday morning, one of his daughters decided to put her dad to the test, although she didn't need him at the time! During a church service, she dialed the private phone number on the platform, no doubt confident that her dad would ignore it and that a staff person would answer the call. To her amazement and embarrassment, her pastor dad immediately responded and upon hearing his child's voice, warmly asked her how he could help her. She froze for a second and then blurted out, "Oh my gosh, it works!" and hung up.

I am not saying that a degree of availability is necessarily required of all parents. But it certainly illustrates that one spiritual leader was determined not to send signals to his children that their needs were unimportant to him.

We all know how therapeutic it is to have times of relaxation and fun with our close friends, whatever our age or stage of life. We come away not only refreshed, but bonded more closely to each other. The same principle works, big time, when we're closely discipling children.

My philosophy says, "The family that prays and plays together, stays together." It sure worked in our family. Jim and I and the kids were crazy about having all-day family picnics and camping holidays together. We took advantage of relaxed times in the outdoors at every possible opportunity. On Friday evenings, even in the winter months, we would take saucepans to the nearest Chinese restaurant, fill them up, take suitable plates and utensils in the car and drive up to the top of a mountain overlooking two harbors in our city.

The view of all the city lights was spectacular. We wouldn't return home until we had walked or run around the nearby mountain trails, singing crazy songs and generally having a ball. Looking back, I see this lifestyle was the perfect balance to the intensity involved in our all-out commitment to know God and make Him known.

If we want our children to be among our closest friends when they grow up, we will need to treat them as close friends when they're in the process. That includes always being loyal to them, courteous, expressing gratitude to them, keeping their confidences, respecting their need for privacy, having fun and recreation with them, sharing their concerns and sorrows, praying with them and listening to them and being approachable and available. Our disciplines in this regard pay enormous dividends later in life—theirs and ours.

Loyalty is a high priority for trust in any friendship. We're not talking about being blindly defensive of the children's failings. That's unrealistic and can be rooted in pride. We need to make sure that we don't fail to acknowledge an offensive behavior in our children that harmed another person simply because we don't want to appear to have failed in any way as a parent.

On the other hand, I have found myself cringing inside when adults openly expose the faults of the children they are discipling—either in front of others or behind their backs. (It usually gets back to them.) Venting this kind of frustration and or anger is extremely damaging to a child's psyche and to the relationship between children and adults.

The Bible leaves us in no doubt as to God's reaction to this unkind, un-Christlike behavior. "Love will *cover* a multitude of sins" (1 Peter 4:8, emphasis mine). If shaming the children, through exposing their sins or shortcomings is the technique being used, we need to recognize that there's a far better way to motivate change.

1. Model the right behavior and react in the opposite spirit from unkindness, which is unconditional love and forgiveness.

2. Keep asking God to bring about the needed changes in the children, and believe He will.

3. Verbally encourage them regarding anything positive in their behavior.

4. Let them know that you're on their side and that you're proud of them.

5. Affirm to them that they are your real friends.

6. Tell them that God has a wonderful plan for their lives, that they are special and precious to God and to you.

7. And tell them that you believe they are going to make a difference in their generation and be mightily used of God, for His glory, regardless of what present shape they are in.

Children desperately need to have that imprinted in their conscious, unconscious and subconscious minds in order to be able to have hope for themselves, let alone to have faith. The enemy's prime tactic is to convince them of everything contrary to those truths. So, pull the rug out from underneath his plans and expose God's plans and purposes. As parents, Jim and I were strong on some of those points listed above, but ignorantly weak on others. As grandparents, we have tried hard to correct our former deficiencies. We live and learn.

History shapers in the making need to have the security of knowing early in the piece about God's absolute justice at all times. When the trials and tribulations come, and no one can escape them, we all need to have strong faith to trust God when we cannot trace Him. The understanding of God's justice greatly contributes to that faith. Those discipling the young can be powerfully used of God to impart the knowledge of this absolutely fair aspect of God's character to them.

If we are confident in hearing God's voice as a way of life, through seeking His face concerning matters large and small, the children under our care will always get a fair deal because we will know how to treat them justly. But if we're going to rely on our own human wisdom, we can act in presumption, judge unjustly and bring severe damage to a child's soul. Tragically, this has been the case history of many innocent children, who, in turn, grow up not being able to trust God's character. I recently heard story after story from a godly, gifted pastor in which he told of being totally misjudged and unjustly mistreated as a child and a young adult, which had left him severely scarred and wounded emotionally. Thank God he was brought to full emotional recovery through in-depth Biblically-based counseling. The following story explains how justice works in everyday family incidents.

One day, when our children were young, I went to use my lipstick and noticed that it was messy and mangled. Upon my inquiring as to which one was responsible, both looked equally innocent and both flatly declared innocence. I said, "Well, Bluey (our family Irish terrier dog) is the only other one who has been in my bedroom, and I don't think she's the culprit." At that point we had total unanimity. I then said, "Do you both think God knows who messed up the lipstick?" Again, 100 percent unity was the affirmative response. "Then I am going into my bedroom alone, shut the door, get down on my knees and ask God to tell me who is responsible, as He knows and I don't. When He tells me, I'll come out and tell you what He says. O.K.?"

"O.K." was the response from both parties. As I knelt, I realized I would have to die to everything I

INFLUENCING CHILDREN TO BECOME WORLD CHANGERS

would logically conclude about the situation in order to hear God's voice, because I wouldn't have a clue why a boy would have any purpose for or desire to use my lipstick. Everything in the natural thinking pointed to the girl.

Then I had to die to all human desire, what I may have wanted the answer to be. Finally, I took authority over the enemy and silenced him in Jesus' name and listened quietly, in expectant faith, for God to speak. In His faithfulness to me and justice to my children, He clearly spoke into my spirit, "It's the boy." I calmly, gently, but firmly delivered the verdict, and the culprit came clean and confirmed the truth of it. (John has given me permission to release this incident, and Jill has said there were other times when her sins found her out!)

The point of the illustration is not to shame dear John, but to tell you that Jill said it made a terrific impact on her as a young child that God was absolutely just and was able to vindicate her when she was innocent. That incident greatly strengthened her faith in God's character.

By the way, you'll be curious, as I was, to know

why on earth John had any use for the lipstick. He and his friend had made some kind of plaything out of wood and they needed some red coloring on their completed masterpiece. Not being able to find a suitable crayon, they resorted to my cosmetics, which produced the desired result.

What about respecting a child's need for privacy? We automatically give that privilege to our adult friends, why not to the children? When our children were small, I assured them that I would not read anything personal that had been written to them, or that they had written to others, or that they had journaled, without their first giving me that privilege by their choices. Nor would I inquire or comment if they didn't. I also assured them that I would not listen in on any conversations they were having with others. In other words, I was simply treating them as friends, and they never needed to fear that I was snooping on them.

At the same time, I made it clear that God knew everything, all the time, that nothing was hidden from His eyes and that He was well able to reveal to me anything that would be harmful to their welfare.

Our daughter is presently the mother of two teenagers. Recently, she told me that the numbers of times I quoted the Scripture verse, "Be sure your sin will find you out," (Numbers 32:23) when she was a child, put the fear of the Lord upon her and kept her from sinning. Decades later, this was encouraging to hear.

THE SINGLE PARENT

God understands the unique challenges and struggles of single parents. And His extra grace and Holy Spirit's enabling is available for each one who chooses to live by the principles in this book. There are numerous case histories to prove it.

We were in our son John's home, where about thirty people had gathered to pray over and commission two vital young people who were about to leave home. One was our grandson, Matthew Dawson, who was leaving for intensive missionary training with overseas outreaches. The other was Rachel Green, the younger daughter of single parent Melody Green. Rachel's sister, Rebecca, had recently completed missionary training by the Kansas City Metro Fellowship, and Rachel was preparing to do the same.

Melody was pregnant with Rachel when her husband, Keith Green, their three-year-old son, and two-year-old daughter were killed in a plane crash. Nothing has been remotely easy for Melody, but she has proved that God is well able to fulfill the spiritual ambitions and answer the many prayers of a faithful, single parent.

My friend, Donnie Eddings, a mother of four children, has also proved God to be *El Shaddai*, the God who is more than enough, in the many inevitable challenging and difficult circumstances of her life as a single parent. Here's her testimony.

One morning I was awakened to the reality that I, a twenty-eight-year-old woman after seven years of a tragic marriage, was now the person fully responsible for the physical, spiritual and emotional needs of my four children. The thought of all this responsibility almost caused me to panic before I picked up my neglected Bible and my eyes landed on "Do not fear, for you will not be ashamed; neither be disgraced, for you will not be put to shame; for you will forget the shame of your youth, and will not remember the reproach of your widowhood anymore. For your Maker is your husband, the Lord of Hosts is His name, and your Redeemer is the Holy One of Israel; He is called the God of the whole earth"(Isaiah 54:4–5).

I know that the context of these verses was God's Covenant of Peace to the children of Israel who were in exile, but for me as a fearful young mother, it became the promise of God that caused me to make the decision which made a drastic change in my life and the lives of my four children.

I had received Jesus Christ as my personal Savior, but I had not made Him Lord over every single area of my life. The idea of His being my husband was totally new and extremely comforting. I said "Lord, I will be the very best mother I can be and I will trust you to be both my husband and the father to my children."

It was then that God directed me to the verse in Psalm 68:5, "A father to the fatherless, a defender of widows, is God in His holy habitation." I knew from that moment that if I would trust the Lord Jesus and His Word, and build my life around Him and what He says, I and my children would have a firm foundation for life.

I did not know at the time that this would involve my moving about fifty miles from my parents and family members to the San Fernando Valley where we would be taught the Bible and have fellowship with others who had committed their entire lives to serving the Lord.

After I was filled with the Holy Spirit, He began to show me all the areas of my life that were not like Jesus. As the process of healing and deliverance took place in me, my children were deeply affected by the drastic change. Consequently, one by one they made their decision to receive Jesus Christ as their personal Savior and made Him Lord of their lives. Each one was then filled with the Holy Spirit.

Today, all of my adult children are witnesses for the Lord Jesus in their respective spheres of influence. My six grandchildren have also committed their lives to the Lord Jesus. Our lives as a family have not been free from tragedy and suffering, but we all know that the source of our strength and fortitude is in God alone.

Due to seeing us walk in this confidence, the children's father, my parents and seven of my eight sisters and brothers have received Jesus Christ as Lord and Savior. Thank you Jesus for proving the reality to me of Luke 17:33. "Whoever seeks to save his life will lose it, and whoever loses his life will preserve it."

I need to add that Donnie Eddings, D.M., has been on many overseas mission assignments in many countries and has led numerous people to Christ. She has also been greatly used of God in praying for people to be physically and emotionally healed and has seen wonderful results.

Now I want to introduce you to one other single parent. Lisa Young was a young mother of four children when I first met her at a retreat where I was speaking in the early 1980s. At that time, she was called of God to intercede for me on a regular basis and has faithfully continued. From time to time she has helped to support my ministry. I am deeply grateful for both these expressions of love. We kept in touch over the years enough for me to know that although Lisa went through a difficult and painful domestic relationship and ended up as a single parent, she was passionately in love with the Lord Jesus. I also knew that she was committed to raising her children in the ways of the Lord.

Therefore, it wasn't too surprising for me to receive a strong prompting of the Holy Spirit to ask her to contribute her testimony related to the subject of this book. But I had absolutely no idea of the extent or impact of this precious woman of God's story until the parts that are relevant to this book arrived in written form.

Lisa has spent untold hours of intercession over many years in the "secret place," hidden away, with the right motive. And the Bible says that when we do that, there will come a day when God will reward us openly. Now is that time for Lisa, and I get the great privilege through this book of bringing about that fulfillment.

I also hadn't any idea of the extent or the depth of how God has used the teaching ministry He has entrusted to me to affect Lisa's life, and in turn, the lives of her four children. I stand back in awe at the work of the Holy Spirit in and through Lisa as she, as much as anyone I know, listened to God's truths from God's Word applied them diligently to her own life and then, as a single parent, prayed, instructed and encouraged her four children to do likewise. In humility, let us learn from one who shares with authority on influencing future history shapers. But before we do, I want to make something very clear.

Both Lisa Young and I have a genuine passion to live solely for the glory of God and are starkly aware that of ourselves we are and can do *nothing spiritual* apart from the life of the Lord Jesus in us and the Holy Spirit's enabling power. We are desperately dependent on both. Therefore, for me to take any credit for the Biblical truths that I applied and then came through me, or how Lisa applied them, is not only totally illogical, it's nauseating. With those facts firmly in place, give glory only to the Lord as you read Lisa's story.

Dear Joy,

First and foremost, I want to thank you for the depth of passion and pain through which your own life messages have been birthed. I understand some of the price. You have laid down your life and the Lord is exponentially multiplying it back to you. Through applying your teachings to my own life, my children (your spiritual grandchildren), have applied and are applying them to their lives with dramatic results.

*I have not veered away from the invaluable wis-
dom by which your messages mentored me, which
started my deeper walk with the Lord as a young
mother. Oftentimes throughout the years, the Holy
Spirit would bring your teachings back to my mind
during my deepest trials, to bring the needed correc-
tion and comfort.*

*Your teachings are not for the faint-hearted, but
for those who have warrior blood in their veins. "No
one engaged in warfare entangles himself with the
affairs of this life; that he may please him who
enlisted him as a soldier" (2 Timothy 2:4). The Lord
has used many of your teachings as a catalyst to
ignite my own spiritual fires as a world changing
intercessor, then as a mother, determined to influence
my four children to become all that God has purposed
for their lives.*

All I can say is, Hallelujah. If the price of obeying God
was for Lisa's testimony alone, it would have been
worth it. And the privilege is always higher than the
price because of who God is.

Lisa continues with her story.

Concerning how to influence future history shapers, I have found it comes first from being entirely sold out to, and zealously in love with, the Lord, as a parent. Secondly, one of my daughters said she was strongly impacted by the countless hours she heard me interceding to God on behalf of others. Thirdly, having a family mission statement also greatly influenced my children. We have based it on Psalm 2:8, "Ask of Me and I will give You the nations for Your inheritance, and the ends of the earth for Your possession," and Deuteronomy 11:24 (KJV), "Every place whereon the soles of your foot treads shall be yours . . . even unto the uttermost sea shall your coast be."

We have applied these scriptures to our lives by praying regularly for the nations of the world,[3] and praying fervently for the different cities in the U.S. where God has placed us, with tangible results. Also, both my youngest daughter and I have separately had the privilege of going on short-term missions trips to several countries in the world.

But probably the greatest influence that has

shaped the lives of myself and my four children has come from hearing your teachings on the fear of the Lord, which motivated me to make a systematic study of every verse in the Bible on that subject. As a result, my whole life is affected by the fear of the Lord (which is to hate *evil [see Proverbs 8:13, emphasis mine])—my personal life, choices, career, ministry, raising my children, prayer life, daily devotions and relationships, just as you taught it would be.*[9]

During this concentrated time of personally studying and applying these truths to my life, the Lord prompted me to share with my children how they could apply different aspects of the fear of the Lord from God's Word to their personal lives in practical ways, as we drove 1.5 hours to school every day. They all did so, with electrifying results, including befriending lonely children in their classrooms. One of my daughters said this family study on the fear of the Lord was the most life-changing time in her spiritual walk with God and was when she first encountered the manifest presence of Christ.

My children have been raised to be culturally unbiased toward people of diverse backgrounds, despite my own sinful past and my prejudiced and racial upbringing. I cannot fully express the jubilant, liberating power of the Holy Spirit in delivering me from that insidious bondage. The fear of the Lord gives us a deep repulsion for all *sin.*

My youngest daughter leads Bible studies at her university, leads and attends all-night prayer rallies, does prayer walks throughout her campus and has been noted by several pastors for her unusually deep insight on the movings and giftings of the Holy Spirit. Before every vacation break, she is always seeking God about the location of her next missions trip.

She and her other sold-out-to-God student friends are praying regularly and fervently for revival on their campus and are some of the most remarkable, on fire, God-fearing young people you could know. All glory to the Lord.

My teenage son was asked to be a youth leader in a large church in New York City. Each school my children attended, they either started a

Christian Club or resurrected a dead one through the power of the Holy Spirit, and they have been called upon by spiritual leaders and high school principals to lead prayer at prayer rallies.

All my children have a deep abiding, healthy respect for God, and when I tell them that "The Lord said," (which I never say lightly) they know and receive it from their Heavenly Father. For example, a few months ago the Lord woke me and prompted me at 3 A.M. to phone my daughter in college and warn her and the other students not to use the "T". This is an underground rail system in Boston. When her housemates woke that morning, she shared the warning and they in turn warned the other students. Although it was a real inconvenience for them to do so, they all heeded the Lord's counsel, which caused my daughter to stand in awe at God's workings and ways.

Shortly after that, we heard from many sources that terrorists were found and taken from the "T" in Boston and the New York subway systems. God's protection and preservation were extended to that entire student body on that campus. God had not only alerted me to the potential danger, but had directed me from many scriptures how to pray for total protection for all students and that the fear of the Lord would be upon them all to heed the word of the Lord. God is so faithful and awesome.

Finally, through your teachings, Joy, I have kept asking God to reveal to me His vision and purposes for us as a family, as well as for each individual child. He has been so faithful to quicken specific scriptures to me, telling me how, when and what to pray for each child, although three of them are now out of the home. These Spirit-directed scriptures have been related to their friendships, intellectual abilities, talents and giftings to each one, provisions, directions, etc. As you have taught, everything we will ever need to know is in God's Word, should He choose to use that method to speak to us.

As a family we are very aware of the truth from Luke 17:10, "So likewise, when you have done all those things which you are commanded, say 'We are unprofitable servants. We have done

*what was our duty to do.'" Our united testimony
is that, by God's amazing grace and through the
power of the Holy Spirit, a single parent, four
children and God are an unstoppable team.*

The bottom line is . . . do we want the children we are
discipling to have a passion for God? Then we will
have to have a passion for Him ourselves and crea-
tively involve them in the hot pursuit. At the same
time we must guard against the error of thinking that,
provided we do everything right, the children will
automatically follow our example and teaching. Each
one has the awesome responsibility of free will and is
ultimately responsible for his or her choices.

As someone once said, "Adam and Eve had the ultimate Parent, in the perfect environment, and they still
chose to rebel."

IT'S NEVER HOPELESS

When we frequently, fervently, and in faith pray for the children we're seeking to influence (the younger the better), in addition to living a consistent lifestyle and providing sound teaching, the chances are high that they will fulfill their God-given destinies as we fulfill ours—in God's way and in God's time.

Proverbs 22:6 says, "Train up a child in the way he should go, and when he is old he will not depart from it." "In the way he should go," means training the child according to Biblical principles. It also implies that because of the uniqueness of each child, there will be a specific plan from God that will enable each one to develop and express his or her personalities and gift-ings, while pursuing their God-ordained destinies. It's not "one size fits all." Seeking God for His wisdom will unfold those plans. For example, in the field of education, a college education may or may not be God's plan for each one. Nothing should be presumed. God's specific plans should be sought by seeking God's face all along the way. Time-consuming? Yes. But infinitely rewarding.

How we pray for children is so important. We should start by relinquishing them into God's hands, asking above all that He be glorified to the maximum in and through them. This means we make no dictations or suggestions as to how He makes them His disciples or through whom He chooses to work. This factor may well be used of God to test us to see whether pride or prejudices surface their ugly heads. God may want to use people of other races or denominations—perhaps the least likely people we would choose. We had better not stand in the way of God's infinite wisdom and knowledge.

We need to take our sticky, possessive hands off the young disciples and have strong spiritual ambition for them to be used mightily of God to affect their generation for the extension of God's Kingdom. To be sent by God anywhere, at any time, under any conditions.

We will get what we pray for, little or much. Never settle for only asking God for the children's conversion to Christ. We should pray persistently towards the large goal with unwavering faith in God's ability to fulfill this vision.

In Galatians 5:6 we are told that faith works through love, so we need to make sure there's no bitterness or resentment in our hearts when we pray.[12] In fact, unconditional love is a top priority according to 1 Peter 4:8: "And above all things have fervent love for one another, for love will cover a multitude of sins." Get the weight of this enormous encouragement: *"Love never fails"* (1 Corinthians 13:8a).

To be Christlike we must be merciful. Mercy is a by-product of love, and it means *not* getting what we deserve. In all honesty, is there any one of us who didn't need God's mercy when we were young? I certainly did. As we keep reminding ourselves of God's unending mercy to us and incredible patience with us, it should cause us to extend the Lord's mercy and long-suffering to the children we're training.

We can either ask God to keep the children we're discipling from trials and difficulties, or we can ask God to make them "strong in the Lord and in the power of His might" (Ephesians 6:10) when faced with the inevitable tests from God, temptations from the enemy and the affects of other people's wrong actions and reactions.

If we have strong spiritual ambition for the ones we are discipling, we will want them to be effective warriors who know how to do spiritual warfare against the powers of darkness.[11] We will ask God to give the children such a large measure of the fear of the Lord that they will fear neither men nor demons, and that they'll be known in heaven and on earth and in hell as those who only fear the Lord.

I was intrigued when a friend of mine shared with me recently concerning an aspect of helping us to understand children better. I knew immediately that it was a wisdom tip from God for this book. She said a friend of hers was having trouble relating to her young son. Wisely, she asked the Lord to help her. The understanding came that she was to lie on her son's bed when he wasn't home and ask God to reveal to her everything from the child's perspective, to show her how he thinks.

It was an illuminating experience, to say the least, as God answered her prayer by giving her insights into why her son reacted in ways that made their relationship difficult at times. This resulted in a change in the mother and then the son—and the relationship difficulties were solved. My friend went on to say that she too followed exactly the same procedure in regard to her son, which produced the same result.

How many more wisdom tips would we all receive if we practiced the art of quietly waiting on God and listening to His advice. After all, He's the original parent and has a vast amount of experience!

When we have consistently done all we know to do, we can be encouraged by these wonderful promises in Jeremiah 31:16–17: "Refrain your voice from weeping, and your eyes from tears; for your work shall be rewarded, says the Lord, and they shall come back from the land of the enemy. There is hope in your future, says the Lord, that your children shall come back to their own border."

If you are struggling with the heartbreaking situation of having children or grandchildren or other loved ones who are not fulfilling their God-ordained destinies, don't give up on God or on them. I have written in a booklet further powerful prayer principles that, when diligently and persistently applied, really work.[6] I know firsthand because I've lived through them over many years and have seen remarkable results.

If you have been praying for a child or a grandchild (or anyone, for that matter) over a long period of time without seeing any results, I don't know a more power-fully encouraging story to share with you than this one. To ensure the privacy of the people involved, I have changed their names. I will refer to the pastor and his wife as Bill and Mary (dear, close friends of mine), and to their son as Don.

As a pastor's son of ten years of age, Don showed no outward signs of the inner rebellion that simmered in his heart against "the whole church thing." It wasn't until he was seventeen that it boiled over and mani-fested itself in his refusal to go to church and ignoring all the household and family rules. At nineteen, Don joined the Navy and things went from bad to worse. He was twenty-one years old, married with one child, when Bill and Mary were notified that their son had disappeared for about a week and was AWOL from the Navy. After searching for him, they found him in San Diego, totally incoherent on drugs and strongly under the influence of demonic spirits.

Pastor Bill was so devastated and distraught that he said, in his own words, "I began to rehearse to God all the things I had done for Him, and yet they didn't produce the expected results in my son's life. I told God I was a complete failure as a father and a pastor, so why should I go on?"

For two weeks Pastor Bill couldn't pray one word, despite the fact that his precious wife Mary would take his hand and gently pray and patiently express her love to him. Bill just went through the motions of carrying out his pastoral ministry.

But God had a plan to meet this dear, disillusioned, angry man. It was on the second morning of a prayer conference he begrudgingly attended. During a time of prayer, Pastor Bill felt the cloud of darkness, created by his unbelief and pride, lift.

Later that day in his own office, a close friend who was concerned about Pastor Bill's spiritual state brought a stranger to Bill. That person embraced him and tenaciously held on to him, repeatedly proclaiming, "God is your only righteousness."

In Pastor Bill's own words:

Each time this phrase was spoken, it penetrated deeper into my heart until I crumpled to the floor. Lying facedown, I wept and asked God to forgive me for my self-righteous attitude. As Father God assured me of His forgiveness, He asked me to look at my hands. Then He asked me, "What spiritual good can come from those hands?" As I pondered, I replied, "Nothing Father, absolutely nothing."

The Lord was showing me that I had been depending upon all the "right things" I had been doing, expecting them to motivate my son to make the right choices. Things like praying, Bible study, self-discipline, having a family altar and serving God. In other words my self-righteousness and my works were the source of my trust, instead of God Himself, who alone could keep my son from the enemy's plans for his life and establish God's plans. Deep repentance and brokenness before God and man brought forgiveness, cleansing, renewed faith, joy, and profound hope for my son and me.

One of the most significant of many promises God gave Pastor Bill concerning his son's returning to the Lord was Isaiah 57:17–18: "For the iniquity of his covetousness I was angry and struck him; I hid and was angry, and he went on backsliding in the way of his heart. I have seen his ways, and will heal him; I will also lead him and restore comforts to him and to his mourners."

As the years went by Don and his wife had three children, and he continued a life of drinking, drugs and promiscuity. For thirteen heartbreaking, long years, Pastor Bill and Mary unconditionally loved, fervently interceded in faith, and waited for God to do what only God can do to bring their son to the end of himself.

It was during a time after his divorce, when Don was on his own in a friend's apartment, that it happened. For several days, Don had been under heavy conviction of sin and had tried to drown it out with heavy drinking and taking drugs, but the conviction remained unabated.

One night, he was woken out of a fitful sleep and became acutely aware of a demonic presence in the room. It was trying to strangle him by the throat and kill him. Don physically wrestled and fought with this demon, knowing this was a matter of life and death. It was only when, with great difficulty, Don managed to call out to the Lord Jesus for help, that the demon took off from his body. At that point Don surrendered his life to the Lord Jesus and asked Him, by faith, to come and live within his heart and cleanse and forgive him for all his rebellion and sins.

At thirty-one years of age, within six months of his conversion, he went to a Youth With A Mission discipleship training school in Hawaii for three months. Then he went on to Bali, Indonesia and participated in a two-month evangelism outreach among the vacationing surfers.

Never, ever give up praying for those unconverted ones. The Hound of Heaven knows how to pursue and reach them. And God has a million ways to do it that we have never heard of or thought of. He is an omnipresent, omnipotent, omniscient, all-loving God. Nothing is too hard for Him.

Perhaps you're realizing how much you've failed in discipling the children God entrusted to your influence and responsibility. Thank God He is bigger than all our failures, knowingly or unknowingly. He's an expert in redeeming any situation, provided that we genuinely humble ourselves and ask forgiveness from God and the ones we have failed. "Who is a God like You, pardoning iniquity and passing over the transgressions of the remnant of His heritage? He does not retain His anger forever, because He delights in mercy. He will again have compassion on us, and will subdue our iniquities" (Micah 7:18–19). That's about as good as news gets. What a God!

As we then exercise faith in God and praise Him for His unending mercy, unfathomable love, unlimited power and ingenious creativity, we can live in the expectation of God's incredible promise in Joshua 3:5, "Sanctify yourselves, for tomorrow the Lord will do wonders among you." I've proved these words in relation to failures during my lifetime.

Our God is the God of the second chance because His mercy is always extended to a truly repentant heart.[7] At any given time, we can start to fulfill the conditions of hearing and obeying God's voice as a way of life.[4] Then we become candidates for influencing potential history shapers and being mightily used of God to extend His Kingdom through the next generations.

THE MASTER MENTOR

I n this last chapter, let's look at how our role model, Jesus, influenced children to become world changers. Because everything about the Lord Jesus amazes and fascinates me, we're bound to make some interesting observations.

Just how important were children to Jesus? Very. He rebuked His disciples for trying to keep the children away from Him. It was very apparent to everyone around the Lord Jesus that He loved the children dearly and wanted to relate to them as friends, not just to tolerate them. How we act and react to children can be a spiritual thermometer of our Christlikeness—or otherwise.

As we consider the following ways Jesus interacted

with children, we will better understand how He influenced them to follow Him.

1) He never hid His genuine affection for them, and loved to have them close to Him, taking them up into His arms (see Mark 10:13–16). The children's response to this unconditional love was to call out with unabashed enthusiasm when in the temple, "God bless the Son of David" (Matthew 21:14–15, TLB). Despite the indignation of the chief priests to this outburst of worship, Jesus totally vindicated them publicly.

Love is so often communicated to a child more by the tone of our voice, the look in our eyes and the gentle way we handle them than by the words we speak or the gifts we give them. Love's arms hate to be empty. The greatest gift we can give children is quality time with them.

It is important to understand that our beautiful Savior, as Son of man, would have longed to have had children of His own. He relinquished that right in order to fulfill His destiny. All those who have been denied the right of parenthood, for whatever reasons, can count on the infinite understanding of the Lord, as described in Psalm 147:5.

2) He totally accepted each individual child without partiality or discrimination. In Genesis 27, we see the damaging results of parents who showed favoritism among their children. Isaac favored Esau. And Rebekah favored Jacob, which resulted in years of hatred and fear among the two brothers. All kinds of insecurities will develop among siblings whenever parents or teachers make comparisons among the children, especially when they are vocalized in the children's hearing.

It is of major importance to strongly affirm to each child the truth that he or she is special and of equal value to God and to the ones who are doing the discipling. So many children grow up feeling overshadowed by a brother or sister who is stronger, better looking, more talented, gets better grades, more athletic, has a stronger personality or is more dedicated to God. It behooves mentors to do all in their power, and through their prayers, to spot the children in those categories and to give them extra, strong encouragement.

Major on anything about them that is unique and enthuse about those aspects.

3) Jesus had strong spiritual ambition for children. Every time He had them in His arms, He blessed them (see Matthew 19:13–15). Oh, that we would understand the power that God releases when we bless children in Jesus' name.

I was deeply touched when I heard my pastor, Dr. Scott Bauer, share that when he was in a supermarket, he saw a little boy from a poor family who looked to be distressed—seemingly an unlikely candidate for having a blessing prayer prayed over him. Obeying a prompting from the Holy Spirit, he smiled at the child and affectionately patted the top of his head and made some friendly remark. Then he silently prayed a powerful blessing over that child's life, a prayer that would impact his future. Pastor Scott went on to say, "Who knows whether that would be the only time that little boy would be blessed in the name of the Lord Jesus."

4) Jesus never turned down a prayer request to heal children. He healed the centurion's servant boy who was paralyzed and dreadfully tormented (see Matthew 8:4–13). He healed the Rabbi's twelve-year-old daughter, who most people thought was dead (see Matthew 9:18–25). He healed the Canaanite woman's daughter, who was severely demon possessed (see Matthew 15:22–28). He cast out a tormenting deaf and dumb spirit from the son of a man who sought His help (see Mark 9:17–27).

5) Jesus repeatedly used little children as examples of how adults were to have the characteristics of childlikeness—first in relation to a basic relationship with the Lord Jesus (see Matthew 18:1–3), and then for spiritual growth (see Matthew 18:4). It is interesting to me that Jesus never used an adult as an example to teach children spiritual maturity.

So, what does it mean to become childlike? Humble, trusting, honest, unself-conscious, obedient, simple (uncomplicated), enthusiastic, able to laugh and cry easily, dependent, submissive, teachable and responsive. In the light of these characteristics, how do we measure up? At a time when Jesus' disciples were asking Him who qualifies to be the greatest in the Kingdom of

Heaven, Jesus immediately called a little child to come to Him and then put him in the middle of the group.

First, Jesus said that no one will make it into the Kingdom of Heaven unless we become childlike. Then Jesus went on to say that whoever humbles himself *as this little child* is the greatest in the Kingdom of Heaven. How did the little child model the humility that impressed Jesus?

First, by his instant, unquestioning obedience to Jesus' command.

Second, by his absolute trust, that having obeyed Jesus it would turn out for his good.

Third, the child stayed put for as long as Jesus needed him, even though Jesus' teaching was lengthy and there wasn't much he could understand. By this he modeled submission and an understanding, that because of who Jesus is, it would be inappropriate to become restless or impatient until Jesus dismissed him. Are these our automatic responses to Jesus' commands at all times?

Finally, Jesus said that if we receive or welcome any little child in His name, like the child he used to model humility, we would be welcoming or receiving Him (see

Matthew 18:5). This should considerably upgrade our view on the importance of ministering Christ's life and love through us to children!

Is it possible that God has wanted to use this little book to change us, as we're seeking Him for answers as to how to change the children for whom we have some regular responsibility?

This would be a good time to repent before God in all honesty, if the characteristics of childlikeness are not evident in us as a way of life. God's Word says in Isaiah 11:6, "A little child shall lead them." In humility, let's follow their example.

6) In John 6:5–14, we see Jesus using a child's gift to meet human need on a large scale. In spite of the disciples' unbelief, Jesus takes what a little guy willingly gives Him in faith and meets the needs of five thousand men besides women and children, through miraculous multiplication. "There is a lad here who has five barley loaves and two small fish, but what are they among so many?" (John 6:9).

My guess is that this same little boy had been around Jesus enough times to know that He had some, if not all, of the above five characteristics. His reckoning would therefore be that the smartest thing he could do was to give Jesus everything he had, and then stand back and watch Him work. We overlook the magnificent faith of this child.

There's no record of the boy worrying about what he was going to eat that day when he gave away all his lunch. There's no mention of his complaining when the disciples took it all away to share it with others. There's no record of unbelief that there was no point whatsoever in giving his little portion to Jesus. No doubt he had watched Jesus in action before and knew that this man was different. There appeared to be no limitations to His ability to fix any situation, no matter how grim or seemingly impossible. May God grant us the humility and faith of this little boy. No wonder Jesus said on several occasions to the crowds, "Get like the children."

7) Jesus issued horrendous warnings to those who would offend children and harm them. If anyone, verbally, physically, emotionally or sexually abuses children, they are inviting God's severe judgment upon themselves. He knows how defenseless the children are and how they are so often trapped by fear of what might happen to them if they ever divulged the truth of the offenses.

Take note of the implications involved with those who tempt young children to sin either by their following the examples of their seniors or by tempting them to be bitter and resentful toward them. Jesus said, "Whoever causes one of these little ones who believe in Me to sin, it would be better if a millstone were hung around his neck, and he were drowned in the depth of the sea" (Matthew 18:6).

If the children who are around us frequently hear us criticizing others, we tempt them to become critical by our bad example. If we are always complaining about something, we tempt them to become ungrateful and moaners. If we are lazy and undisciplined, we tempt them to be slothful. If we are bad tempered and display rage, use foul language and operate deceitfully, we provoke and tempt them to copy us. The list is endless.

If on the other hand, we have chosen to "grow in grace and in the knowledge of our Lord and Savior Jesus Christ" (2 Peter 3:19) as a way of life, we will attract them to that pathway of love, light and liberty. By our lives we will be provoking the children nearest to us to make the right choices which will inevitably shape their futures and influence them to fulfill their God-ordained destinies. What an awesome privilege, responsibility and opportunity.

8) In Matthew 18:10, Jesus further emphasizes His loving, caring concern for the children, understanding the vulnerability of their dependence upon adults. Father God has a built-in protection to cover the helplessness of little children. He has provided guardian angels in Heaven who keep their eyes on God so that when He who is everywhere, has all knowledge, and all power sees the need for the children's help, He immediately dispatches angels to go into action on their behalf.

In fact, Jesus starts the sentence with a warning, "Beware that you do not despise or feel scornful toward or think little of one of these little ones" (AMP). Again, Jesus is emphasizing the enormous value He places on each little child.

When our grandson Matthew was three years of age, he disappeared from John and Julie's family when they stopped during a car journey on a winter's evening to have a meal at a restaurant in a sparsely populated area. Each parent thought Matthew was in the care of the other one. Upon discovering his absence, they all started calling his name and searching diligently through the surrounding scrub area outside the restaurant, praying fervently for Divine intervention. It was dark.

When John's flashlight finally shone on his precious little boy, Matthew simply said, "A man came and touched my shoes and I couldn't do anything but sit down here. I couldn't walk." There wasn't any sign of a man in that area of low scrub. God made it very clear to John and Julie and their two other boys that God had dispatched Matthew's guardian angel to keep him from running farther away. Their response of deep gratitude and relief was praise and worship to our Heavenly Father who neither slumbers nor sleeps and who is on duty twenty-four hours of every day to rescue His children.

Whatever the Lord Jesus has pronounced to be of great significance to Him and His Kingdom purposes, Satan has a counteracting plan to destroy. This is evident by the fact that, around the world, untold millions of babies each year are murdered through abortions. The world has been deprived of the potential of millions of outstanding history makers and shapers in this generation.

If we really love God, we will be committed to cooperating with Him in the extension of His Kingdom worldwide. That inevitably includes doing everything within our power, and being diligent, fervent and persistent in our prayers for two things to happen. First, that all pregnant women will have the revelation that what God has sovereignly allowed to be created in their wombs, is a special treasure from Him, with limitless possibilities of bringing glory to His name and further extending His Kingdom. Pray also that they will understand that responsibilities, privileges and opportunities come with the package.

Second, that if they sincerely believe that giving their privilege of parenthood to someone else would be in the best interests of the child, that they would be willing to relinquish their rights and hand the newborn baby over to the parents of God's choosing. God, in His faithfulness, will clearly direct anyone who seeks

Him diligently in faith. His Word says, "I will instruct you and teach you the way you should go; I will guide you with My eye" (Psalm 32:8). There are untold numbers of couples praying, waiting and yearning to have the opportunity and responsibilities of parenthood. In God's justice, love, mercy and grace, He always has a plan to fulfill the needs of every human being who submits to His Lordship.

We only find that plan through having the humility expressed in the submission, dependence, trust and unconditional obedience of a little child. That's when Jesus takes us up in His arms and blesses us with the clear directions and solutions to every problem, in His way and in His time. That's when Satan's destructive plans are thwarted, leaving him and his demons confused and frustrated.

So, whose side are we on? Can't be on both!

Please remember that if you are undecided about what to do or what advice to give concerning a child in a mother's womb, think about the great value God places on that child. In Jeremiah 1:5, God speaks to the young prophet Jeremiah and says, "Before I formed you in the womb I knew you; before you were born I

sanctified you; I ordained you a prophet to the nations."
The baby Jeremiah, while still in the womb of his
mother, was set apart by God for His service, and his
life's ministry defined. Think about that!

Then in Psalm 139:13–16 (TLB), David shares the
wonder of God's miraculous methods of forming his
being while still in his mother's womb, and ends up
basking in the comforting fact that God is thinking
about him all the time.

> You made all the delicate, inner parts of my body,
> and knit them together in my mother's womb.
> Thank you for making me so wonderfully complex!
> It is amazing to think about. Your workmanship is
> marvelous—and how well I know it. You were
> there when I was being formed in utter seclusion!
> You saw me before I was born and scheduled each
> day of my life before I began to breathe. Every day
> was recorded in your Book!

Listen to God's comforting, encouraging, all-
encompassing promise given to those who decided to
live God's way, from God's Word, with God's enabling

grace. "For I know the thoughts that I think toward you says the Lord, thoughts of peace and not of evil, to give you a future and a hope" (Jeremiah 29:11).

Now, dear reader, I have tried to give you enough understanding of God's priorities in relation to influencing children to become radically real, like Jesus, in the hope that you will settle for nothing less in your interactions with them.

As I come to the close of this book, I want to make something crystal clear. While a lot of my family illustrations are related to missions, it does not mean that I think the message of this book is better illustrated through those who are missionaries. That just happens to be what we are as a family by God's sovereign choice.

My earnest prayers, for decades, have been and still are, that in *every sphere of society,* in every nation, God would raise up those who would pay the price to be used of Him as world changers.

Be assured, my prayers are with you in our united pursuit to "raise the bar" of the standards, so that we who are involved in discipling children will be better equipped to influence them toward fulfilling their God-ordained destinies. By so doing, the history of the world will be further shaped until " . . . the kingdoms of this world have become the kingdoms of our Lord and His Christ, and He shall reign forever and ever!" (Revelation 11:15).

Dear Reader,

Because of the subject matter of this book, I understand that there may be people who would want to write me requesting prayer and/or counsel related to problems with their involvement with children. Please understand that THERE IS NO WAY I CAN MEET THAT EXPECTATION and fulfill God's priorities for my life.

The purpose of this book has been to share with you proven Biblical principles that, when you apply them in your circumstances, you will in time discover they work for you, too.

You will need to go to other sources for any further counsel and prayer. I am counting on your understanding and cooperation.

Very sincerely and warmly,

JOY DAWSON

APPENDIX
RESOURCE GUIDE

1. Joy Dawson's message on this subject is obtainable from her Resource Guide; audio tape # JD-98.
2. For instruction on this subject, see Joy Dawson's book, *Intercession, Thrilling and Fulfilling*, chapters 8 and 9.
3. A complete listing of all the nations is at the back of Joy Dawson's book, *Intercession, Thrilling and Fulfilling*.
4. For instructions on how to hear God's voice, see Joy Dawson's book, *Forever Ruined For the Ordinary: The Adventure of Hearing And Obeying God's Voice*.
5. For more teaching on this subject, see Joy Dawson's Resource Guide, audio tapes # JD-71, JD-84, JD-145, JD-154.
6. For teaching on this subject, see Joy Dawson's booklet, "How to Pray for Someone Near You Who Is Away from God."
7. For teaching on the mercy of God, see Joy Dawson's Resource Guide, audio tape # JD 45.

8. For an expanded teaching on this subject, see Joy Dawson's booklet, "The Character of the One Who Says, 'GO.'"

9. Joy Dawson's teaching on the fear of the Lord is in her book, *Intimate Friendship with God through Understanding the Fear of the Lord*. It is also in her video tape series # JDV-5, JDV-6, JDV-7, JDV-8, JDV-9, plus an audio tape series of five tapes, # JD-88 through JD-92.

10. See teaching on spiritual warfare in Joy Dawson's book, *Intercession, Thrilling and Fulfilling*.

11. For an expanded teaching on this subject, see Joy Dawson's book, *Forever Ruined For The Ordinary*.

12. For powerful, practical teaching on how to come to complete forgiveness see Joy Dawson's Resource Guide, audiotape # JD-36.

All these resources are obtainable from
Y.W.A.M. 11141 Osborne St.
Lake View Terrace, CA 91342.
Phone (818) 896-2755, Fax (818) 897-0738

E-mail: info@ywamla.org
Web site: www.ywamla.org

ABOUT THE AUTHOR

J OY DAWSON's Bible teaching ministry and missionary journeys have taken her to fifty-five countries around the world. In addition, multitudes have been blessed by her extensive television and radio ministry and countless lives have been changed through the international distribution of her audio and video tapes. The character and ways of God are the biblical basis of her penetrating teachings, which cross denominational lines. She is the author of the bestselling books *Forever Ruined for the Ordinary; Intimate Friendship with God; Intercession, Thrilling and Fulfilling;* as well as *Some of the Ways of God in Healing.* Joy's booklets are *Knowing God, How to Pray for Someone Away from God,* and *The Character of the One Who Says "GO."*

Hear Joy Dawson teach on almost 200 different key subjects.

Ideal for: Training Schools, Bible Institutes, churches, home groups, private study.

Resource Guide

With many new additions

Life-Changing Books · Videotapes Audiotapes

By Joy Dawson

Since 1970 Joy Dawson has ministered extensively around the world as a Bible teacher and conference speaker, and has authored a number of books. Her penetrating teachings are based upon the character and ways of God. Multitudes have found them to be life-changing. Her missionary journeys have taken her to fifty-five nations. Joy and her husband Jim, along with their two married children and six grandchildren are with Youth With A Mission. They all live in Southern California.

LOS ANGELES

Youth With A Mission
11141 Osborne St., Lake View Terrace, CA 91342
Phone (818) 896-2755 Fax (818) 897-6738
E-mail: YWAMLA@compuserve.com
WEBSITE www.ywamla.org

Send your name and address to:

**Youth With A Mission
11141 Osborne Street
Lake View Terrace, CA 91342, U.S.A.
Phone: (818) 896-2755 Fax: (818) 897-6738
Email: info@ywamla.org
Website: www.ywamla.org**

Other titles by Joy Dawson...

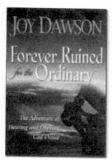 This exciting book explains how to experience the adventure of hearing and obeying God's voice as a way of life.

 An inspiring manual taking the reader to greater depths and breadth in effective prayer for others.

This insightful best seller explains how God's standards of holiness affect every area of our lives.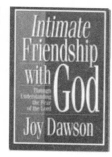

If you have more questions than answers about healing then this book is for you. Joy is ruthless in her pursuit of truth from God's Word.

Booklets...

 Powerful insights in prayer that cause God's hand to be moved on behalf of others.

 THE CHARACTER OF THE ONE WHO SAYS "GO."

This booklet deals with aspects of God's character that makes us secure in Him when we obey the Great Commission of Mark 16:15

 This booklet reveals the paramount importance of our understanding the many facets of God's fascinating character, and the multiplicity of His ways.

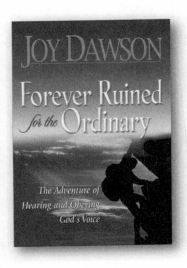

Joy Dawson describes what happened when she decided to follow God with an obedient heart: "I was tuned in and turned on to God, the Creator and Sustainer of the universe. I took off on an adventure of a lifetime . . . hearing and obeying God's voice. I was forever ruined for the ordinary."

Emphasizing God's commitment to be personally involved in our lives, Joy shares the lessons of a lifetime of faithful obedience to God. Through stories and biblical teaching, she helps readers discover the excitement of learning how to listen to God, joyfully obey Him, and see the wonder of the results that follow.

ISBN 0-7852-6682-8

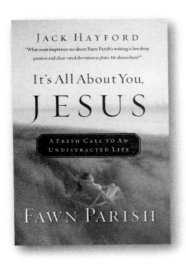

In modern Christendom, religious catchphrases and spiritual slogans abound, but too often these buzzwords are a smoke screen for lives without substance. At best, they are the peripherals that threaten to overshadow the one thing we truly need . . . more intimacy with Jesus.

In *It's All About You, Jesus,* Fawn Parish offers fresh insight on the distorted emphasis on worship in our churches and how we can change it. Readers will learn how to make Jesus the focus of every aspect of their lives. For those yearning to experience deeper intimacy with a living Savior, and for those desiring to effectively change the way they worship, *It's All About You, Jesus* is required reading.

ISBN 0-7852-6612-7